BIBLE VISUALS international

Helping Children See Jesus

ISBN: 978-1-64104-021-1

A Kingdom Forever
Old Testament Volume 23:
Kings, Chronicles Minor Prophets Part 1

Author: Katherine E. Hershey
Illustrator: Vernon Henkel
Computer Graphic Artist: Kristen Hall
Page Layout: Morgan Melton, Patricia Pope

© 2018 Bible Visuals International
PO Box 153, Akron, PA 17501-0153
Phone: (717) 859-1131
www.biblevisuals.org

RELATED ITEMS

To access related items (such as activities, memory verse posters and translated texts) please visit our web store at www.biblevisuals.org and enter 2023 at the top right of the web page. You may need to reduce the zoom setting to get the search box.

FREE TEXT DOWNLOAD

To obtain a FREE printable copy of the English teaching text (PDF format) under Product Format, please scroll down and select Extra–PDF Teacher Text Download. Then under Language select English before clicking the ADD TO CART button to place in your shopping cart. Other languages are available at an additional cost from the Language menu. When checking out, use coupon code XTACSV17 at check-out and click on Apply Coupon to receive the discount on the English text.

Wisdom
Riches
Honor

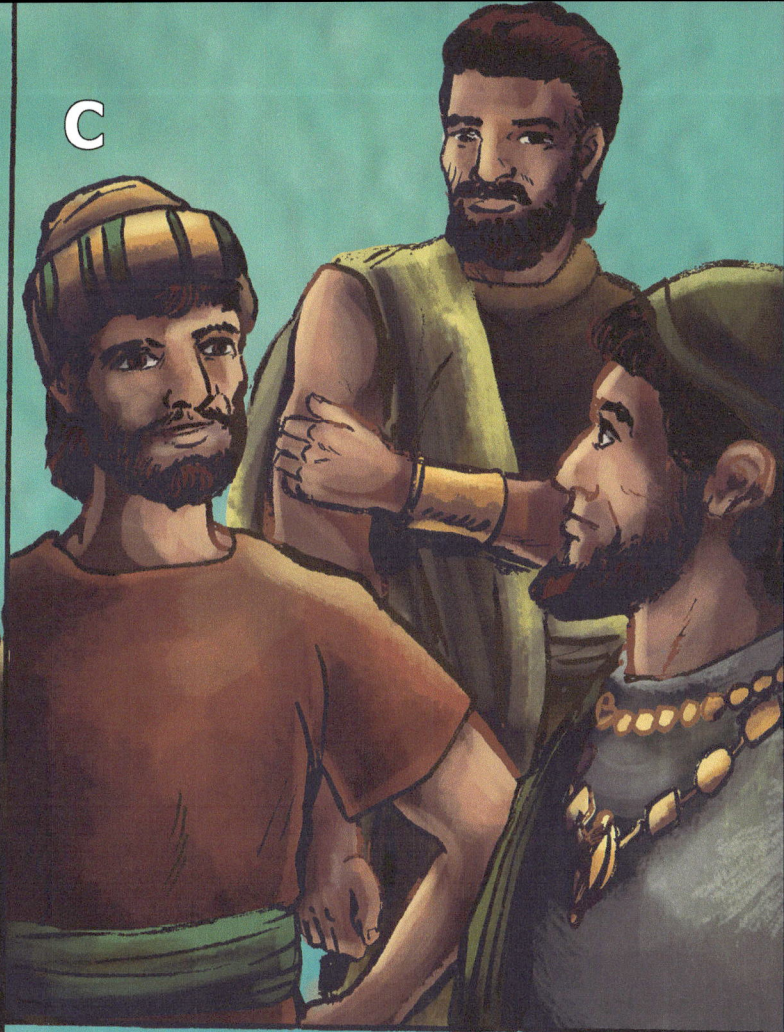

Sidon

PHOENICIA

Damascus

ARAM

Mediterranean Sea

ISRAEL
Northern Kingdom

Shechem

Ramah

Jerusalem

JUDAH
Southern Kingdom

The Kingdom Torn Apart

MOAB

PHILISTIA

EDOM

EGYPT

The Temple

SYRIA
(Aram)

• Damascus

LEBANON

Tyre •

ASHER

• Dan

NAPHTALI

ZEBULON

Sea of
Galilee

East
MANASSEH

ISSACHAR

Jordan River

MANASSEH
• Dothan
ISRAEL
(Northern Kingdom)
• Shechem

GAD

EPHRAIM

• Bethel

DAN BENJAMIN

✡ Jerusalem

Mediterranean Sea

Dead Sea

REUBEN

JUDAH
(Southern
Kingdom)

SIMEON

EGYPT

– 17 –

All that is in the heaven and in the earth is Thine; Thine is the kingdom, O LORD, and Thou art exalted as Head above all.

1 Chronicles 29:11b

Scriptures to be studied: 2 Samuel 7:11-29; 1 Chronicles 17:1-27; 22:2-23:1; 28:1-29:13; 2 Chronicles 1:2-10; 1 Kings 1:33-40; 2:1-4; 3:4-15

The *aim* of the lesson: To show that God's plans are always best.

What your students should *know*: God's plans for the kingdom and the temple.

What your students should *feel*: A willingness to allow God to change their own plans.

What your students should *do*: Give the Lord first place in their lives.

Lesson outline (for the teacher's and students' notebooks):

1. David's desire (1 Chronicles 17:1-27; 2 Samuel 7:11b-29).
2. David's instructions (1 Chronicles 22:2-23:1; 28:1-19; 29:1-13; 1 Kings 2:1-4).
3. Solomon crowned king (1 Kings 1:33-40; 3:4; 2 Chronicles 1:2-6).
4. Solomon Instructed (1 Kings 3:5-15; 2 Chronicles 1:7-12).

The verse to be memorized:

All that is in the heaven and in the earth is Thine; Thine is the kingdom, O LORD, and Thou art exalted as Head above all.　　　　　(1 Chronicles 29:11b)

NOTE TO THE TEACHER

The books of Kings and Chronicles contain important historical information. From these books we learn this: The success of each king depended upon his obedience to God's law. Obedient kings had successful nations Kings and nations which disobeyed the law of God were punished.

The books of Second Samuel, Kings, and Chronicles are continuous and interwoven. However, some facts are duplicated. We learn much of David's life from 2 Samuel. His death is recorded in 1 Kings 2:10-11. David's ancestors are listed in 1 Chronicles 3:1-16. The details of the remainder of his life are in 1 Chronicles 11:1-29:30. Thus we begin this series in Chronicles.

Remember: A good lesson is more than teaching history. It must also affect your students' lives. In this study we learn the importance of accepting God's plans. Examine your own heart, Teacher. Does God have first place in *your* life?

THE LESSON

Think of something you would most like to do. Think hard! . . . But wait a minute. Would your choice be different if God was first in your life? (Allow brief discussion.)

King David remembered a time when he wanted to do something for God. Do you suppose the Lord let him do it? Listen carefully.

1. DAVID'S DESIRE
1 Chronicles 17:1-27; 2 Samuel 7:11b-29

David was old now. He sat thinking about his past life. He smiled when he remembered his victory over the giant Goliath. He had been young then. But with one stone, he killed the giant who hated God's people. How was this possible? He wholly trusted the Lord God.

David also had sad memories. After he killed Goliath, King Saul became jealous of him. Several times the king tried to get rid of David. Often David had to run and hide from the king. But David loved God and usually trusted Him. More than anything else, he really wanted to please the Lord. God almost always had first place in David's life.

Show Illustration #1

David also remembered when he–King David–planned to do something special. He had talked about his plans with Nathan, the prophet. (Good prophets, like Nathan, spoke for God.) David had said, "Nathan, I am living in a beautiful palace. But the ark of the Lord is in the tabernacle (a movable tent)." David wanted to build a magnificent building for God's ark.

The ark of God was a box made of wood, covered with gold. (Point to top left of Illustration #1.) The lid, called the mercy seat, was made of solid gold. On each end of the mercy seat was a golden cherub. The cherubs (like angelic beings) had wings which spread over the mercy seat. (*Teacher:* If you have Volume 10 of this *Visualized Bible* series, show illustration on page 9.)

The ark of the Lord stood in the holiest place of the tabernacle. The cloud of God's glorious presence hovered above the ark. (Compare Exodus 40:35 with 1 Kings 8:10-11.)

The prophet Nathan had agreed with David. God indeed should have a magnificent house where He could be worshiped. (Point to top right of Illustration #1.) But that night God spoke to Nathan. "David is not to build a house for Me," God said. "I have been among My people and have moved with them in a tent. Tell David he is not to build a house for Me. But I shall build a house for David."

What did the Lord mean–"I shall build a house for David"? God told Nathan to explain it to David this way: "When you die, your son will become king. When your son dies, his son will become king. When that son dies, his son will become king. I, the Lord God, shall set up David's kingdom forever." That was what God meant when he said, "I shall build a house for David." He meant a *family*. He had chosen David's family to be a family of kings forever.

The next morning Nathan had gone to King David. "O King, I am sorry," he said. "I was wrong. God does not want you to build a house for Him."

"Why not?" David asked.

Nathan explained, "God says *He* will build a house for *you*. After you die, your son will become king. God's kingdom will be set up through your family. The house God will build for you, David, is your family. And this is God's promise: 'Your son will be the one to build a beautiful house for Me.' "

David had been disappointed, for he wanted to build God's house. But he was satisfied. He knew God's plans are always best.

Much had happened since that day. David was old now. Soon his son, Solomon, would be king.

2. DAVID'S INSTRUCTIONS
1 Chronicles 22:2--23:1; 28:1-19; 29:1-13; 1 Kings 2:1-4

One day King David had a long talk with his son. "Solomon," David said, "I wanted to build a house–a temple– for God. Because I am a man of war, God would not let me build it. But you, Solomon, will be a man of peace. (See 1 Chronicles 22:7-9.) God told me, 'Your son will build My house.'"

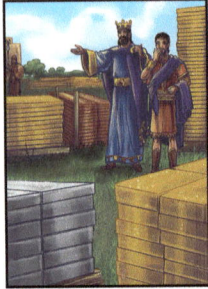

Show Illustration #2

King David said more: "I have been getting things ready for the temple. I have made plans for the building. I have collected gold, silver, iron, bronze, and much fine wood."

When Solomon saw everything, it took his breath away. There were tons and tons of gold and silver! There was more bronze and iron than could be weighed! King David explained how the materials were to be used. He gave Solomon the completed building plans for the temple. "Solomon," he said, "the people will help with all the work."

Then King David spoke to the leaders of the people. "My son is young and inexperienced. [Solomon was about age 20.] The temple to be built for the Lord should be exceedingly magnificent. It must be famous and splendid in the sight of all the nations" (1 Chronicles 22:5).

King David gave orders to the leaders saying, "Help Solomon. Give yourselves to the Lord your God. Get to work. Build the temple in Jerusalem. Then bring the ark of the Lord into it." The leaders were to give God first place.

The people were delighted when they heard the news about the temple. So they willingly gave gold and silver and precious gems. God's people also chose to give Him first place in their lives. Oh, how happy they were!

Anyone who places God first, has real happiness. But not everyone gives God first place. Why not? Because many are separated from God because of sin. Each one must believe that God's Son died on the cross. When Christ Jesus died, He took the punishment for our sins. (See Romans 6:23; 1 Peter 2:24.) If you will receive Christ as your Saviour, you will become God's child. (See John 1:12.) You will be a member of the family of God. Then you can let Him change your plans. "Give God first place." This was good advice for those who gave materials for the temple. It is good advice for us.

Finally King David said, "Solomon, I am going to die soon. You will then be king. You must be strong and careful to obey God. Walk in His ways. Keep His commands. Then you will prosper in all you do. Listen carefully now! The Lord gave me this wonderful promise: 'If you and your family will always walk in My ways; and if they walk truthfully with all their heart . . . then a man of your family will always be on the throne of Israel'." (See 1 Kings 2:4.)

God wanted Solomon to know this: He, his sons and grandsons should always put God first. Then they would have continual blessing–and happiness–from the Lord God.

The Lord wants us, too, to have His blessing and happiness. We shall never be kings. But we can have the joy of obeying God and giving Him first place.

3. SOLOMON CROWNED KING
1 Kings 1:33-40; 3:4; 2 Chronicles 1:2-6

Show Illustration #3

Before King David died, Solomon was crowned king. The trumpet sounded. The people shouted, "Long live King Solomon!" It was a happy, happy day! One called, "May the Lord be with Solomon! May He make Solomon's throne even greater than David's!" (See 1 Kings 1:37.) David would die. But God had chosen Solomon as the new king. David's kingdom would go on.

Soon afterward, Solomon called the leaders of Israel together. It was a large crowd for Israel was a great nation. Solomon and all the people went to the tabernacle. The tabernacle was the large movable tent (see Exodus 36-38) built hundreds of years before. (You have never seen such a tent!) The Bible says Solomon "offered a thousand animal sacrifices" at the tabernacle. We cannot imagine so many animals being sacrificed. There Solomon and the people would have confessed their sins.

Those sacrifices are a picture of the sacrifice of the Lord Jesus. He, God's Son, gave His life on the cross. His sacrifice was far greater than any animal sacrifice. He offered Himself– one sacrifice for sins *forever*. He died, arose, and went to Heaven. His work was finished. So He sat down at God's right hand (Hebrews 10:10, 12). Because Christ paid for our sins with His blood, we can have forgiveness. Animal sacrifices like those Solomon offered, are no longer needed. Indeed, God will no longer accept them.

4. SOLOMON INSTRUCTED
1 Kings 3:5-15; 2 Chronicles 1:7-12

After Solomon offered those sacrifices, God spoke to him in a dream. "Ask for whatever you want Me to give you," God said.

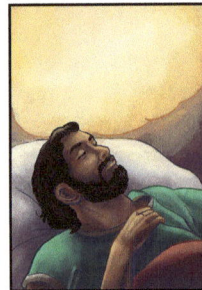

Show Illustration #4

Listen to Solomon's answer. "O Lord, You have shown great kindness to my father David. He was faithful to you. Now, O Lord, You have made me king in place of my father. But I am like a child. I do not know how to rule these people. There are more of them than can be counted. Give me wisdom and knowledge so I shall know what to do. Help me to understand what is right and what is wrong . . .

Do you think Solomon's answer was a good one? (Encourage response.)

God thought Solomon's answer was good. Listen to what the Bible says: "The Lord was pleased that Solomon asked for wisdom." (See 1 Kings 3:10.)

So God told Solomon, "You asked for wisdom. But you did not ask to be rich and famous. You did not ask for the death of your enemies. Nor did you ask for long life. So I have given you what you asked: A wise and understanding heart. You will be the wisest man who ever lived. And I will also give you riches and honor." (*Teacher:* On Illustration #4, print WISDOM, RICHES, HONOR.) God continued, "While you live, Solomon, no king will be as great as you. If you will walk in My ways . . . if you obey My commands (as your father David did) then I shall give you a long life."

We do not need the wisdom Solomon needed to be king. But we must be wise. We must have wisdom to make the right choices. We need to know how to do right. God's Word says: "If anyone lacks wisdom, let that person ask of God. He gives liberally to all" (See James 1:5.)

Do you really want to obey God? Do you want the Lord to have first place in your life? If you do, will you tell Him so right now?

Have you received the Lord Jesus as your Saviour from sin? If not, you can do so now. Tell God you have sinned. Tell Him you believe the Lord Jesus died for your sin. Receive the gift of eternal life Christ provides. If you truly believe, He will forgive your sin.

Lesson 2
GOD'S GLORY IN SOLOMON'S KINGDOM

NOTE TO THE TEACHER

Study earnestly these portions of Scripture. Imagine that you yourself are right there. Think of seeing the stacks of wood for the temple. How would you have felt, looking at the gold, silver, and gems? Catch the thrill of observing the magnificent temple. What would have happened in your heart when God's glory cloud came down? Suppose you saw those thousands of sacrifices consumed with fire from God. It really, truly happened. Teacher, make the truths live to your students. Help them to have the thrill of being in the center of the action.

In this lesson, we learned the importance of worshiping God. We worship the Lord by acknowledging His worth.

The more we know about Him, the more we appreciate His worthiness. Your own spirit of worship, Teacher, should carry over to your students.

In our last lesson, the emphasis was on putting the Lord first. Ask your students to tell their experiences in giving God first place.

In this lesson, emphasize that "God alone is worthy of worship." Do you (or your students) love anything more than God? Whatever is more important than God, is an idol. And the Lord God of Heaven hates idolatry.

Scripture to be studied: 1 Kings 5:1-6:38; 8:1-60; 9:1-10:9; 11:1-43; 2 Chronicles 2:4-3:2; 5:1-14; 6:1-21; 7:1-22

The *aim* of the lesson: To teach the importance of worshiping God.

What your students should *know*: The reason for God's command to worship Him alone.

What your students should *feel*: A desire to please God through true worship.

What your students should *do*: Worship only the true and living God.

Lesson outline (for the teacher's and students' notebooks):

1. Solomon builds the temple (1 Kings 5:1-6:1, 11-14, 38b).
2. Solomon dedicates the temple (1 Kings 8:1-6, 10-21; 2 Chronicles 5:1-14).
3. Solomon's blessing and prayer (1 Kings 8:22-60; 9:1-9; 2 Chronicles 6:1-7:1-3, 12-22).
4. Solomon's greatness, his failure and death (1 Kings 9:26-10:9; 11:1-11, 41-43a).

The verse to be memorized:

All that is in the heaven and in the earth is Thine; Thine is the kingdom, O LORD, and Thou art exalted as Head above all. (1 Chronicles 29:11b)

THE LESSON
1. SOLOMON BUILDS THE TEMPLE
1 Kings 5:1--6:1, 11-14, 38b

Suppose you had lived in Bible lands about 2500 years ago. There is one place you would have wanted to see–the city of Jerusalem. (Point to Jerusalem on back cover map.)

David's son, Solomon, was the new king. Important, beautiful buildings were being built. There was a greater

palace for the king. In it were a throne room, a big storehouse, and much more. It would take 13 years to build that big palace! (See 1 Kings 7:1-12.) Another building which particularly thrilled the Jewish people was the temple of God.

You should know about God's temple.

King Solomon had sent a message to his friend, King Hiram. (Hiram was the king of Tyre–point to Tyre on map.) King Solomon said to King Hiram: "My father (David) wanted to build a temple for the worship of God. But there were many wars in my father's time. So God would not let him build it. (See 1 Chronicles 27-10; 28:3.) The Lord told my father, 'Your son will build My temple.' Now there is peace in my kingdom. So I am planning to build God's temple."

King Solomon continued, "But I would like to have your help, King Hiram. We need wood from your excellent forests. Your men are experts at cutting timber. Will you have them chop down trees for us? I shall pay whatever wages you ask. My men will work with yours."

King Hiram was delighted! "Praise be to the Lord!" he said. "God has given David a wise son to rule over this great nation" (1 Kings 5:7, 12). He then sent this word to Solomon, "I shall provide all the wood you want. My men will haul the logs from the Lebanon forests to the Mediterranean Sea. I shall float the logs on rafts to whatever city you choose." Imagine all that wood afloat on the Mediterranean Sea! [The wood would be received at the temple site in Jerusalem.] King Hiram added, "You can pay me, King Solomon, with food for my royal household."

The agreement pleased both kings. King Hiram sent loads of wood. And King Solomon paid him with thousands of bushels of wheat and barley. He included more olive oil and wine than you can imagine. (See 2 Chronicles 2:10.) Solomon continued to do this for King Hiram year after year. Hiram had many, many people to be fed!

Show Illustration #5

King Solomon needed much more than wood for his magnificent temple. For example, he had to have huge blocks of stone. So he ordered, "At the stone quarries, cut the stones to the exact size." His men obeyed. Each stone was measured and trimmed perfectly. We read in God's Word, ". . . No hammer, chisel or any other iron tool was heard at the temple site while it was being built" (1 Kings 6:7).

Many thousands of people worked on the temple. Some of them used gold, silver, bronze and iron. The inside walls, the floor, the carvings were covered with real gold. Even gold nails were used in one part of the temple! (See 2 Chronicles 3:6-10.) Beautiful jewels and precious gems helped make the building "magnificent."

It took seven years to build God's temple. Suppose you had been 10 years old when the building began. You would have been age 17 when it was finished! (*Teacher:* Use ages of your students.)

Finally the temple work was completed. But the most important furnishing was not there. The ark of the Lord was needed. Without it, the temple was only a splendid building.

2. SOLOMON DEDICATES THE TEMPLE
1 Kings 8:1-6, 10-21, 27, 30; 2 Chronicles 5:1-14

King Solomon called for certain men. "Go get the ark of the Lord," he commanded. (Show ark, Illustration #1, top left. For details of the ark, see Exodus 25:10-22; 37:1-9.)

The priests carried God's ark, as the Lord had taught them. They did not touch it. (See Numbers 4:15.) Long poles went through rings on the sides of the ark. The priests carried the covered ark by the poles. (See Numbers 4:5-6.) The holy ark was never seen except by the high priest. And he saw it only once a year. (See Hebrews 9:7.) Now crowds on the city streets watched as the covered ark passed. The ark was a reminder that God was with His people. What a happy day that was!

The priests brought God's ark to the temple courtyard. There King Solomon stood with thousands of the Israelite people. They sacrificed more sheep and oxen than could be counted. And they worshiped the Lord God of Heaven.

The animal sacrifices pictured ahead of time the sacrifice of Christ Jesus. He is the perfect Lamb of God.

Then the priests took the ark into the most holy place. The precious old, old ark was now in the magnificent new temple! Inside the ark were two priceless stone tablets. (See I Kings 8:9.) The Lord Himself had written His commandments on those tablets. (See Exodus 31:18.) God's first two commands were these: "You shall have no other gods before Me. You shall not make for yourself any idol. You shall not bow down to idols nor worship them." (See Exodus 20:3-5.) This means that people then, and we today, are to worship God alone. He is the only true and living God.

Finally the priests left the most holy place.

Show Illustration #6

In the courtyard, the priests joined the musicians. Trumpeters (120 of them!) along with other instrumentalists, played their praise to God. And singers sang: "God is good; His love lasts forever." (See 2 Chronicles 5:12-13.) Oh, how the singers sang! They gave praise and thanks to the Lord in their songs.

The Lord God, watching from Heaven, was pleased. His thick glory cloud came down. God's glorious presence filled the temple, just as it had filled the tabernacle. (See Exodus 40:34; 2 Chronicles 5:14.)

3. SOLOMON'S BLESSING AND PRAYER
1 Kings 8:22-60; 2 Chronicles 6:1-7:3, 12-22

The Israelite people were amazed to see God's glory cloud. The Lord Himself was with His people. King Solomon turned and blessed them. He spoke of what the Lord had done for them. (See 2 Chronicles 6:1-11.)

Show Illustration #7A

Then the king knelt on a specially built bronze platform. Raising his arms to Heaven, he prayed aloud and worshiped God. "O Lord," he began, "there is no God like You in Heaven above or on earth below." King Solomon understood that God is high above all others. No one can ever compare with Him! The king thanked the Lord for His faithfulness. He said, "You, Lord God, have kept Your promise about this temple. You fulfilled Your promise today." (See 1 Kings 8:23b-24.) The king asked for God's continued presence and protection. (See 1 Kings 8:25-30.) He prayed that if ever God's people sinned, He would forgive them. (See 1 Kings 8:30, 34, 36, 39, 50.) Always, however, the people were to confess their sins to God.

Surely you praise God. Do you also worship Him? Do you tell Him how much He means to you? Do you show by your words that you respect and honor Him? Is the Lord more important to you than anything or anyone else? Have you told Him so? Do you confess your sins to Him? Asking for forgiveness of sin was included in Solomon's worship.

The king ended his prayer saying: "Lord, be with us . . . May we walk in all Your ways. May we obey Your commands . . . May all people everywhere know that You, Lord, are God . . . There is no other." (See 1 Kings 8:57-60.)

Then Solomon and all the people offered thousands and thousands of animal sacrifices.

Show Illustration #7B

And "fire came down from Heaven and completely burned the sacrifices" (2 Chronicles 7:1). Did you hear that? God immediately accepted all those sacrifices which His people offered to Him! And again, "the glory of the Lord filled the temple." The God of Heaven was with His people. "When all the Israelites saw the fire coming down and the glory of the Lord above the temple, they knelt . . . and worshiped and gave thanks to the Lord, saying, 'He is good; His love lasts forever' " (2 Chronicles 7:3).

Right then God spoke to King Solomon. "I have set apart this temple . . . by putting My Name there forever," God said. "My eyes and My heart will always be there." The Lord God would always have His eyes on His people. He would love them with His heart. God continued, "Now, Solomon, do right and obey Me. If you do, I shall set up your kingly throne forever. But do not turn away from Me. Do not worship idols. If you do, I shall remove My people–the Israelites–from this land. And I shall destroy this temple." (See 1 Kings 9:3-9.)

Surely Solomon would always worship only God the Lord.

4. SOLOMON'S GREATNESS, HIS FAILURE AND DEATH
1 Kings 9:26-10:9; 11:1-11, 41, 43a

King Solomon became one of the greatest kings of all time. People everywhere heard about him and his riches. Kings and queens came from far away. They wanted to see if all they had heard was true. And it was. This made the Lord God more important to them, too.

God had special rules for the kings of His people. They were not to copy the kings of other nations. And also, God's kings were *not* to have: (1) many horses; (2) many wives; (3) much money. (See Deuteronomy 17:15-20.)

The time came when Solomon disobeyed all these rules. And many of his wives worshiped idols!

Now listen to these sad words from the Bible:

"As Solomon grew old, his wives turned his heart after other gods. His heart was not fully devoted to the Lord his God . . . Solomon did evil in the eyes of the Lord. He did not follow the Lord completely . . . And the Lord became angry with Solomon . . . (See 1 Kings 11:4, 6a, 9a.)

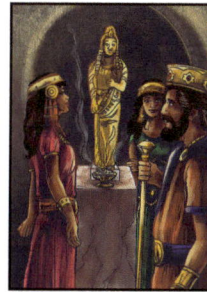

Show Illustration #8

Solomon's wives worshiped idols. Then Solomon turned to idols. And the Lord God was angry.

God said, "Solomon, you have not walked in My ways. You have not obeyed Me. You will be punished." (We shall learn about his awful punishment in our next lesson.)

Solomon was king for a long time–40 years. For many of those years he obeyed the Lord. Then Solomon sinned greatly. No longer did God have first place in his life.

You may not have sinned as Solomon did. But God's Word says, "All have sinned." You cannot truly worship God until your sin is forgiven. God's Son, the Lord Jesus Christ, gave His own precious blood for your sin. Will you place your trust in Him? If you will receive Him as your Saviour, He will forgive you.

Have you already placed your trust in the Lord Jesus? If so, you will want to worship the true and living God. You do not need a temple. You can worship Him right here, or wherever you are. (See John 4:20-24.) Remember! Worship is telling God how worthy He is of our love, respect, and all that we have. Worship is praising and thanking God for who He is. Will you worship Him right now?

(*Teacher:* Allow time for students to worship the Lord aloud.)

Lesson 3
THE KINGDOM TORN APART

NOTE TO THE TEACHER

The Lord God, maker of Heaven and earth, can do as He chooses. Early in history, He chose the man Abraham to father a great nation. One of Abraham's grandsons, Jacob, was later called Israel. (See Genesis 32:22-28.) Jacob's 12 sons became known as the Israelites. Their families grew so large that each family formed a tribe. Those 12 tribes were known by the names of their fathers. (See back cover map with tribal names.)

God chose a particular land in which Abraham and his descendants would live. That land (Canaan) finally became known as Israel. The Lord promised that the land would be Israel's if they obeyed Him. He warned them *not* to worship idols. If they disobeyed and turned from Him, they would lose their land.

From the beginning, the Lord was King of His people. But the time came when the Israelites wanted a king they could see. Neighboring nations had kings. So the Israelites (God's chosen people) wanted to be like other nations. And the lord chose to let them have their own way. First there was King Saul. King David was next, followed by his son, Solomon. King Solomon was a good king at first. But he turned to idol worship. So God chose to tear apart the nation of Israel. Wicked Jeroboam ruled over ten northern tribes. This larger Northern Kingdom kept the name Israel.

Solomon's son, Rehoboam ruled over the two tribes in the south. This Southern Kingdom used the name of its larger tribe, Judah. At first, Rehoboam was a good king. Later "he did evil because he had not set his heart on seeking the Lord" (2 Chronicles 12:14). The people God had chosen for Himself, chose to go their own way. They refused to follow God's directions.

Study carefully the Scriptures covering this lesson. The tearing apart of God's Kingdom was a dreadful day in Israel's history. God's people abandoned Him. But He has never, never forsaken them–or us!

Interestingly, King Rehoboam chose the city of Shechem for his coronation. The Lord had first appeared to Abraham in Shechem. There God promised to give the land of Canaan to His people (Genesis 12:6-7). Later Jacob lived in Shechem (Genesis 33:18-20). And Joseph was buried there (Joshua 24:32). When the Israelites entered their land, at Shechem they dedicated themselves to obey God's Law (Joshua 24:1-27). Shechem was, therefore, important to the Israelites.

Remember the very important rule of good teaching; **review**, review, review.

Scripture to be studied: 1 Kings 11:43-12:33; 14:21-31; 2 Chronicles 10:1-11:17; 12:1-16

The *aim* of the lesson: To show the importance of following God's directions–not the advice of others.

What your students should *know*: That the tearing apart of God's Kingdom caused the 10 northern tribes to:

(1) abandon the temple worship; and (2) follow Jeroboam's false worship.

What your students should *feel*: A desire to follow only God's directions.

What your students should *do*: Ask God today for His directions.

Lesson outline (for the teacher's and students' notebooks):

1. Rehoboam crowned king (I Kings 11:43-12:20; 2 Chronicles 10:1-15).
2. God's Kingdom torn apart (1 Kings 12:16-24; 2 Chronicles 10:16-11:17).
3. Jeroboam worships idols (1 Kings 12:25-33).
4. Judah's sin and God's punishment (1 Kings 14:21-31; 2 Chronicles 12:1-16).

The verse to be memorized:

All that is in the heaven and in the earth is Thine; Thine is the kingdom, O LORD, and Thou art exalted as Head above all. (1 Chronicles 29:11b)

THE LESSON

Long ago God gave many directions to His people, the Israelites. His directions were always for their good. He directed them how to worship. The people of Israel knew they were to worship God at the magnificent temple. They understood that to worship the Lord is to honor and respect Him. They worshiped Him when they prayed and when they sang. Their songs spoke of the marvelous God of Heaven. The Lord knew the hearts of those who truly worshiped Him. He saw who loved and followed His directions.

When Solomon became king, he really wanted to obey God's directions. What did he first ask the Lord to give him? (*Teacher:* Encourage response.) King Solomon asked for wisdom. And the Lord gave him wisdom. So Solomon knew God's way and could have become a great king. He received many wonderful gifts from the Lord. But King Solomon began to love the gifts more than God. He had received wisdom from the Lord. But he refused to live wisely. He no longer followed God's directions.

Indeed, King Solomon was so disobedient that he made the Lord angry! (See 1 Kings 11:9-13.) God told him, "I shall tear the Kingdom away from you, Solomon. I shall give a large part of it to one who serves you. But I shall not do it in your lifetime. I shall do it during the life of your son."

Think of it! God wanted David and his family to have the whole Kingdom forever. Now, because of Solomon's sin, the Kingdom would be torn apart. And God Himself would do the tearing.

Later, one of King Solomon's men, Jeroboam, met a prophet of God. (See 1 Kings 11:28-31.) The prophet took off his new coat and tore it in 12 pieces. He said, "Jeroboam, take 10 pieces for yourself. The Lord God says, 'I am going to tear the Kingdom away from Solomon.' And God will give you, Jeroboam, ten of the 12 tribes." (*Teacher:* Show map on back cover. Point to names of tribes.)

God explained that the other two tribes would remain with Solomon's family. (See 1 Kings 11:32-40.) The city of Jerusalem was on the border of those two tribes. God had chosen to be worshiped at Jerusalem.

Jeroboam looked at the ten pieces in his hand. He thought, *Ten tribes of the Kingdom will be mine. The prophet of God said so. But how can I ever become king?*

The time came when King Solomon died and was buried in Jerusalem. (See 1 Kings 11:41-43.) And Solomon's son, Rehoboam, would be the new king. (*Teacher:* Have students repeat Jeroboam's and Rehoboam's names frequently.)

1. REHOBOAM CROWNED KING
1 Kings 11:43-12:20; 2 Chronicles 10:1-15

Rehoboam went to Shechem (show map), a city which was important to the Israelites.

Show Illustration #9A

In Shechem the people crowned Rehoboam king. The trumpeters blew their horns. The people shouted, "Long live King Rehoboam!" They promised, "We shall serve and obey you, King Rehoboam!" How happy they were!

After a while, one man began to cause trouble for King Rehoboam. Can you guess his name? Jeroboam was the man!

Show Illustration #9B

He and others had been talking. "King Solomon made everything hard for us," one said. "He took our sons and daughters to be his servants. And he made us pay him lots of money (taxes). Our taxes are much too high!" Together the men agreed, "Our taxes are too high!"

So Jeroboam, along with a big crowd, went directly to King Rehoboam. One man began, "Your father, King Solomon, made life hard for us. We will support you if you promise to make life easier. Do not take so many of our people to be your servants." Then they all shouted, "And cut our taxes!"

King Rehoboam ordered, "Come back in three days for my answer."

Show Illustration #9C

The king called for some of his older men. He told them what the people wanted. "What is your advice?" the king asked.

"Do what the people said," the men answered.

Show Illustration #9D

King Rehoboam was not satisfied. He called some young men (his own age). He told them what the people demanded. "What should I do?" he asked. Instead of asking *God* for directions, the king asked *people* for advice. The young men gave this answer: "Tell them you will make life harder than your father did! You will take more of them to be your servants. You will add to their taxes. And say this: 'My little finger is thicker than my father's waist!' Then they will know how powerful you are!"

Three days later Jeroboam and his men came to King Rehoboam. The king spoke harshly to them. "I am going to make life harder for you. And I shall raise your taxes!"

This made the Jeroboam crowd angry. "Rehoboam, what do we have to do with you?" they shouted. "We are done with King David and his family! We are going home! Look after your own house, O David!" They turned their backs on King Rehoboam (David's grandson) and stomped out!

So Jeroboam became King Jeroboam of the 10 northern tribes. This part of God's Kingdom was called Israel. (*Teacher:* Have your students frequently repeat the locations and names of the two kingdoms and their kings.)

2. THE KINGDOM TORN APART
1 Kings 12:16-24; 2 Chronicles 10:16-11:17

Show Illustration #10

King Rehoboam went home to Jerusalem down south. Jerusalem was in the tribe of Judah. So that part of God's

Kingdom became known as Judah. God's wonderful Kingdom was torn apart! Was the Lord God surprised? Oh, no! (*Teacher:* Read 1 Kings 11:11, 30, 31; 2 Chronicles 10:15.)

The magnificent temple was in Jerusalem. Solomon had built it originally so all 12 tribes could worship God. Now only two tribes worshiped there. In time, many people from the Northern Kingdom moved down to the Southern Kingdom. They wanted to be near God's temple. So they went to Judah, King Rehoboam's kingdom. The Bible says, "Those from every tribe of Israel, who set their hearts on seeking the Lord," came to Jerusalem (the capital city). (See 2 Chronicles 11:16-17.) Because of this, Judah, the Southern Kingdom, became strong.

3. JEROBOAM WORSHIPS IDOLS
1 Kings 12:25-33

King Jeroboam lived in Shechem, the capital of the Northern Kingdom. (Point to Shechem on map, page 10. Later the capital was moved to Samaria.) King Jeroboam was worried. He thought, *My people are going down to Judah to worship in God's temple. Soon they will turn to King Rehoboam and kill me. What should I do?*

Who had chosen Jeroboam to be king? (Let students answer.) God Himself! God had promised Jeroboam great blessing if he would obey the Lord. (See 1 Kings 11:31-39.) But Jeroboam neither obeyed nor trusted God.

So, instead of asking the Lord for directions, he turned to men. He said, "Many people are going down to the Southern Kingdom to worship. What shall we do?" Together they finally made a decision.

Show Illustration #11

King Jeroboam made two golden calves. He placed one in the northern part of his Northern Kingdom at the city of Dan (see back cover map). The other calf was placed in the south, in Bethel. He called the people together. "It is too much for you to go to Jerusalem to worship," he said. "See these gods, O Israel . . ."

Did you hear that? He called the golden calves "gods"! God had commanded, "You shall have no other gods before Me. You shall not make any graven image." Jeroboam knew God's Law. But he did not obey it. What a dreadful sin!

The Northern Kingdom people followed King Jeroboam. They worshiped the golden calf idols instead of the true and living God. The Bible tells us, "Jeroboam sinned and made Israel to sin." (See 1 Kings 14:16.) And this was only the beginning! Twenty-one times after this, the Bible speaks of bad kings. Each one was "like Jeroboam who caused Israel to sin."

4. JUDAH'S SIN AND GOD'S PUNISHMENT
1 Kings 14:21-31; 2 Chronicles 12:1-16

King Rehoboam in the Southern Kingdom (Judah) became strong. But after a few years, he too turned from the Lord. Rehoboam and many of his people worshiped idols.

Then God allowed the king of Egypt to capture many of Judah's cities. (*Teacher:* See the size of Egypt's army–2 Chronicles 12:2-4.) In Jerusalem, King Rehoboam and his leaders were terrified! A prophet of God warned them, "The Lord says this: 'You have left Me. So I now leave you to the king of Egypt.'" King Rehoboam and his men knew God did right in punishing their sin. So they humbly turned to God and asked His forgiveness. And guess what happened. The Lord forgave them. He really, truly did! (Check 2 Chronicles 7:14.)

Show Illustration #12

But God let the Egyptians take marvelous treasures of gold from His magnificent temple. The Lord allowed it because His people had turned to idol worship. This is sin. And sin must be punished.

There was continual war between the Northern and Southern Kingdoms. (See 2 Chronicles 12:15.) Think of it–God's very own people fought against each other. At last King Rehoboam died. Of him, God's Word says, "He did evil, because he had not set his heart on seeking the Lord" (2 Chronicles 12:14). God struck King Jeroboam and he also died (2 Chronicles 13:20). Both men had led God's people to worship idols. Awful, awful sin!

God punished sin in the long ago. And sin must be punished today. All people everywhere have sinned. But the Lord Jesus took our punishment for sin by dying on the cross. (See 1 Peter 2:24.) Have you turned to Him for forgiveness? Have you received Him as your Saviour from sin? When you receive Him, He receives you as His child forever. (See John 1:12.)

Do you belong to the Lord? If so, God is willing to give you directions for living. (See Proverbs 3:5-6.) Will you ask Him now to direct you *today*?

Lesson 4
GOD'S KINGDOM IS FOREVER

Scripture to be studied: 2 Samuel 7:11-16; 1 Kings 11:11-13; 1 Chronicles 17:11-14; 2 Chronicles 14:1-16:14; Deuteronomy 28:1-15, 58-65; Luke 1:26-33; Zechariah 14:9; Revelation 11:15

The *aim* of the lesson: To show that God will keep His promise of a lasting Kingdom.

What your students should *know*: That God's Word will come true: His promises *and* His warnings.

What your students should *feel*: Happy anticipation of being a part of God's unending Kingdom.

What your students should *do*: Make certain they have accepted God's promise of eternal life.

Lesson outline (for the teacher's and students' notebooks):

1. The Kingdom as it had been promised (2 Samuel 7:11-16; 1 Chronicles 17:11-14)
2. The Kingdom and God's warnings (1 Kings 11:11-13; Deuteronomy 28:1-15, 58-65).
3. The Kingdom as it had become (2 Chronicles 14:1-16:14).
4. The Kingdom which will come (Luke 1:26-33; Zechariah 14:9; Revelation 11:15).

The verse to be memorized:

All that is in the heaven and in the earth is Thine; Thine is the kingdom, O LORD, and Thou art exalted as Head above all. (1 Chronicles 29:11b)

THE LESSON

Have you ever waited for a promise to come true? Maybe your parents once promised you something. They said, "You may have it when you are old enough." Or, "You will get it when you can take care of it." Maybe you did something wrong which kept your parents from keeping their promise. You knew they would be true to their promise. But when?

1. THE KINGDOM AS IT HAD BEEN PROMISED
2 Samuel 7:11-16; 1 Chronicles 17:11-14

Show Illustration #13

(*Teacher:* Print the name of one king on each crown: DAVID, at top followed by SOLOMON, REHOBOAM.)

God had promised King David, "You will have a kingdom forever. When you die, your son will be king. I shall set up the throne of his kingdom forever. If he sins I shall punish him. But your family and your kingdom will be forever."

Later, God made a promise to Solomon. The Lord said, "Walk in My way as David your father did. If you do, I shall set up your kingdom forever. I made this promise to your father David: 'You will never fail to have a man on the royal throne of Israel.' But, Solomon, do not turn away from Me. If you or your sons worship idols, punishment will follow." (See 1 Kings 9:3-7.)

At first Solomon worshiped only the true and living God. Later he turned from God to idols.

After Solomon died, his son, Rehoboam, became king. For a while, King Rehoboam obeyed the Lord. But, like his father, he also turned to idols. Then God punished him dreadfully. What was God's punishment? (*Teacher:* Encourage student response.)

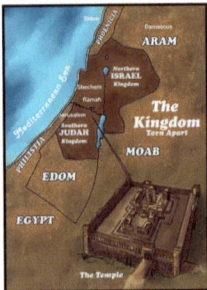

Show Illustration #10

God's wonderful Kingdom was torn apart. God would not let Rehoboam (from David's family) rule over the whole kingdom. He was king of only a small part in the south.

2. THE KINGDOM AND GOD'S WARNINGS
1 Kings 11:11-13; Deuteronomy 28:1-15, 58-65

That the kingdom had been torn apart was no surprise to God. But how would He keep His promise of a "kingdom forever"?

From the beginning, God wanted His people to live in their own land. It was the land He had given them. They could live there if they obeyed Him. They could not live there if they worshiped idols. Once He spoke of the future of His people. The Lord commanded: "Obey Me! If you do, I shall set you above all nations of the earth . . . You will be the head, not the tail. You will be at the top, never at the bottom."

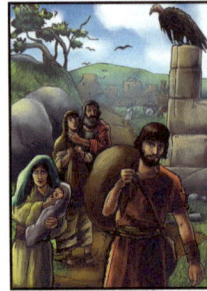

Show Illustration #14

"Do not turn away from My commandments. If you disobey Me, I shall scatter you among all nations. You will be spread from one end of the earth to the other." (See Deuteronomy 28:13-14, 58-64.)

After Solomon sinned God warned him: "I shall not take the kingdom from you while you live. I shall take part–but not all of it–from your son. I shall keep My promise to David. Men from David's family will rule in Jerusalem." (See 1 Kings 11:9-13.)

Why, oh why, did the people God had chosen for Himself, disobey Him? Why did they refuse to listen to His warnings? Why did they insist on worshiping idols? The Lord wanted the best for His people. But they wanted their own way. How would God keep His promise to them? How would there be a Kingdom forever?

3. THE KINGDOM AS IT HAD BECOME
2 Chronicles 14:1-16:14

In time Asa (David's great, great grandson) became the new king of Judah, the Southern Kingdom. King Asa loved the true and living God. He hated idol worship.

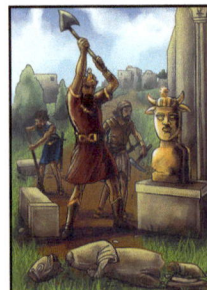

Show Illustration #15

So in every town he smashed all the idols and altars. He commanded the people: "Seek the Lord God of your fathers! Obey God and His laws!" The people did what King Asa said. Therefore, the Lord blessed King Asa and Judah with peace. They had no enemies, so there were no wars in the Southern Kingdom. Instead of fighting, they built strong cities with high walls.

King Asa had only a small army. The soldiers were brave because they trusted the Lord. One day a huge army marched against Judah. The enemy army had twice as many soldiers as Judah. And they had 300 chariots! King Asa led his army to the battlefield. There he turned to the Lord. Asa prayed, "Lord, there is no one like You. You can help those who have no power. Help us, O Lord our God. We rely on You. In Your Name, Lord, we have come against this huge army. O Lord, You are our God. Do not let men have victory over You."

The Lord heard the king's prayer. He struck the enemy, crushing their army! (See 2 Chronicles 14:11-13.) It was a miracle! God Himself won the victory for good King Asa and his soldiers.

The people of Israel (the Northern Kingdom) saw that God was with Judah (the Southern Kingdom). Because of this, many God-loving Israelites moved down to Judah. In Jerusalem the people of Israel joined Judah in worshiping the Lord. They all had a great celebration. (See 2 Chronicles 15:9-14.) Oh, how they loved the Lord!

Up in the Northern Kingdom (Israel), the new king, Baasha, was very unhappy. He did not like it that many people had gone to Judah. So he called his builders together. "We'll build a fort at Ramah," he announced. (Ramah was near Jerusalem, capital city of the Southern Kingdom. *Teacher:* Show map on page 10.) "We shall make it big and strong," King Baasha said. "Then no one will be able to leave or enter Judah."

When King Asa heard this, he was afraid. So he took silver and gold out of the Lord's temple and the palace. He sent it to a neighboring ungodly king. [Ben-Hadad in Damascus.] This king and King Baasha were friends. But King Asa used the Lord's silver and gold to bribe Baasha's friend! "Break your agreement with King Baasha," King Asa said. When Baasha's friend saw the silver and gold, he turned against Baasha. And he made this agreement with King Asa: "I shall fight with you against King Baasha!"

The bribe had worked. But the Lord was not pleased. He sent a prophet to King Asa. A prophet tells God's message. "Why did you go to a king who does not love God?" the prophet asked. "You trusted the Lord when that huge army came against you. And God did a miracle. Your small army won the victory. This time you did not trust the Lord. So from now on, you and all Judah will be at war."

King Asa hated the prophet's message. So he turned against the prophet and threw him into prison. How foolish it is to become angry with someone who speaks God's message! It is possible to keep the messenger quiet. But that does not change God's message. What God says must come true.

The Bible says King Asa was a good king. And he was, except this time when he failed to trust God. Sometimes we Christians also fail the Lord. But He is ready to forgive us. This He does when we confess our sin to Him. (See Proverbs 28:13; 1 John 1:9.)

King Asa died and was buried in Jerusalem. His son became the new king of Judah, the Southern Kingdom.

Of the kings of Judah, we read this: "The king died. And his son became king." There were 19 kings in Judah, the Southern Kingdom. And always the kingdom went from father to son. The kingdom was kept in the family of David.

It was different with the Northern Kingdom, Israel. Of the 19 kings there, less than half were sons of kings. The kings didn't stay in the same family. Why? Because they had turned to idol worship. And God tore His Kingdom from them.

Why did kings of Judah, the Southern Kingdom, remain in the same family? Because God had made a wonderful promise to King David. "Your family and your kingdom will be forever." And so it was for a long time (about 250 years).

Now listen carefully: David's family is not ruling in Jerusalem now. So what happened to God's promise?

The Lord had sternly warned His people. "If you will not obey Me," God said, "you will be taken from your land. You will be scattered among all people. You will be spread from one end of the earth to the other." (See Deuteronomy 28:62-64.) God's people in the Southern Kingdom did not obey Him. So His warning came true. Enemy nations marched into the land of Judah. All Jerusalem was destroyed. The king and people were taken to another land. You will learn more about this in coming lessons. Years later, a few of God's people returned to Jerusalem. They did some rebuilding. But they did not have a king. Enemy nations ruled over them. And God's own special people were scattered in other lands.

4. THE KINGDOM WHICH WILL COME
Luke 1:26-33; Zechariah 14:9; Revelation 11:15

Hundreds of years went by. Still there was no word from God about the promised kingdom. God's punishment seemed greater than His promise. Then one day God spoke again. This time He spoke through the angel Gabriel to a young woman, Mary. And Mary was from the family of David! The angel said, "Mary, you have found favor with God. You will have a Son and will call His name Jesus."

Now listen carefully to the angel's next words. "He will be great and will be called the Son of the Highest. And the Lord God will give to Him the throne of His father David. He will reign over the house [the *family* or *nation*] of Jacob [Israel] forever. His kingdom will never end."

Here again was God's promise! There is going to be a kingdom forever. And Jesus Christ the Lord will reign over God's Kingdom. (See Revelation 11:15.)

Show Illustration #16

Some future day the Lord Jesus Christ will return to earth. He, Jesus, God's Son [David's greatest Son], will come to the city of Jerusalem. There He will be crowned King. And there will be peace on the earth. (See Psalm 72:7-8; Daniel 7:13-14; Zechariah 9:10; 14:9.) Because the Lord Jesus knows everything, He will reign perfectly. (See Isaiah 11:2-5.)

That will be a glorious time on earth. "For the earth shall be filled with the knowledge of the glory of the Lord, as the waters cover the sea" (Habakkuk 2:14). And there will be peace on the earth. ". . . Nation shall not lift up sword against nation, neither shall they learn war any more" (Isaiah 2:4). Then "the kingdoms of this world will become the kingdoms of our Lord, and of His Christ. And He shall reign forever and ever" (Revelation 11:15).

Teacher: Let the minds of your born-again students be over-joyed with the anticipation of that glorious day. If you have unsaved students, close with the following.

The Lord Jesus is not ruling from a throne in Jerusalem now. He has not been crowned King. The only crown He wore here on earth was a crown of thorns. The people refused to have Him as their King. (See John 1:11; 19:15.) So they crucified Him.

Of course, this was no surprise to God. Indeed, it was all in His plan. In His message to Joseph through the angel, God promised: ". . . Jesus . . . will save His people from their sins" (Matthew 1:21). For people to be saved from sin, Jesus, God the Son, would die. When He died on the cross, He took the punishment for your sin and mine. (See Ephesians 1:7.)

Will you place your trust in Him? If so, you can be sure of forgiveness of sin. (See Acts 10:43.) He can forgive you because His death was not the end. He rose again and lives in Heaven. Will you thank Him for dying for you?